W9-AAC-106

EMT

CRISIS CARE FOR INJURIES AND ILLNESS

Tom Greve

Rourke
Educational Media
rourkeeducationalmedia.com

Scan for Related Titles and
Teacher Resources

Before & After Reading Activities

Level: **Q**   Word Count: **888 Words**
100th word: *boy page 5*

Before Reading:

Building Academic Vocabulary and Background Knowledge

Before reading a book, it is important to tap into what your child or students already know about the topic. This will help them develop their vocabulary, increase their reading comprehension, and make connections across the curriculum.

1. *Look at the cover of the book. What will this book be about?*
2. *What do you already know about the topic?*
3. *Let's study the Table of Contents. What will you learn about in the book's chapters?*
4. *What would you like to learn about this topic? Do you think you might learn about it from this book? Why or why not?*
5. *Use a reading journal to write about your knowledge of this topic. Record what you already know about the topic and what you hope to learn about the topic.*
6. *Read the book.*
7. *In your reading journal, record what you learned about the topic and your response to the book.*
8. *After reading the book complete the activities below.*

Content Area Vocabulary
Read the list. What do these words mean?
catastrophes
dispatcher
distress
efficiency
emergency
rural
technician
trauma
triage
undergo

After Reading:

Comprehension and Extension Activity

After reading the book, work on the following questions with your child or students in order to check their level of reading comprehension and content mastery.

1. *Describe what the primary job of an EMT is.* (Summarize)
2. *Why do you think the need for EMTs is going to increase in the future?* (Infer)
3. *Can you think of a time when you needed an EMT?* (Text to Self Connection)
4. *Why are EMTs referred to as first responders?* (Asking Questions)
5. *What is the first thing you would do if you needed the service of an EMT?* (Visualize)

Extension Activity

On a piece of poster board, draw a picture of your home. Using colored markers, label each room and map out an evacuation route that shows the nearest exit from every room. Have your parent check smoke alarms and make sure you have a fire extinguisher available in case of an emergency. Go over your evacuation plan with everyone in your family and do a practice drill to make sure everyone understands. Then, place your poster in an obvious place within your house.

TABLE OF CONTENTS

Warm, morning sun shines on a school playground. Children happily shout and laugh as they run, swing, and climb. Suddenly the laughter turns to nervous silence amid one child's cries of pain. A little boy has fallen from the monkey bars. It is an **emergency**. His leg is broken!

It is important not to move an injured person until an EMT arrives to figure out how severe the injury might be.

The boy's teacher sees he is seriously hurt and cannot walk. Using a cell phone to call 9-1-1, the teacher asks a **dispatcher** for help. Within moments, the wail of a siren rises and an ambulance arrives. Out rushes a specially trained Emergency Medical **Technician**, or EMT, who comforts the boy and begins treating his injured leg. Minutes later, the boy is in the ambulance headed for treatment at a hospital.

Every day, millions of people go visit a doctor because they are not feeling well, or they are hurt.

Sometimes, however, people are too sick or too hurt to get to their doctor. Like the little boy with the broken leg, they need help right away, wherever they are. That is when EMTs spring into action.

EMT Levels

LEVEL ONE: BASIC TRAINING

EMT: Person has met basic training requirements and can provide first aid, basic emergency medical care, and can transport patients.

LEVEL TWO: INTERMEDIATE TRAINING

EMT: Person is licensed as a basic EMT and has had additional medical training.

LEVEL THREE: ADVANCED TRAINING

EMT/Paramedic: Person has completed advanced medical training, can give medicine to patients in **distress**, and perform certain life-saving procedures on the way to the hospital.

EMTs respond to many kinds of emergencies from playground accidents to fires and even crime scenes. Whatever the emergency, an EMT responds with quickness and **efficiency**. Some people call EMTs the rescue squad.

EMERGENCY FACT

If you or someone you are with is seriously hurt, use a telephone to call 9-1-1. The dispatcher will need to know where you are and what happened so he or she can send EMTs to help you.

EMERGENCY FACT

In most U.S. cities and large towns, EMTs work as part of the local fire department. In many **rural** areas, fire departments and emergency medical workers are volunteers.

The men and women who serve as EMTs travel in ambulances, fire trucks, and sometimes helicopters. Anywhere emergency help is needed you'll find them. They are brave and selfless in difficult situations. But, before they can be efficient helpers in an emergency, EMTs have to **undergo** special medical training.

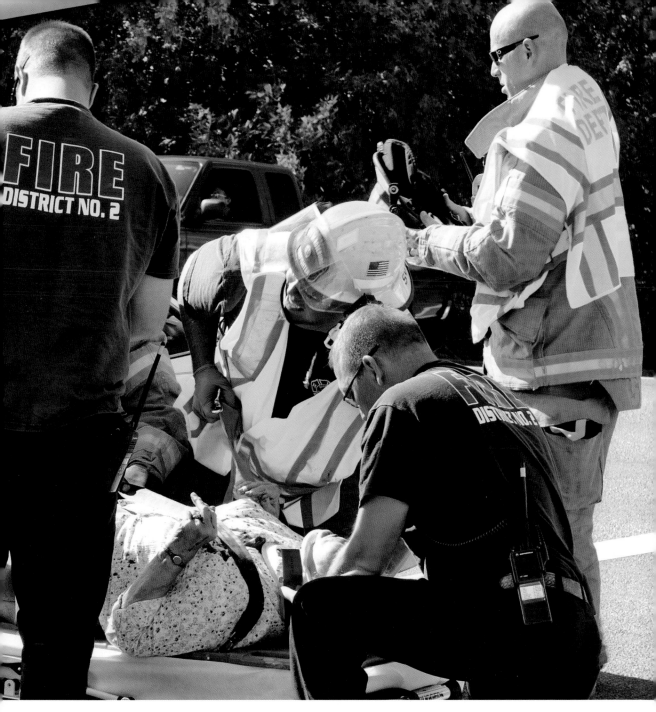

EMTs often work alongside paramedics. EMTs and paramedics are not doctors. Their job is to help injured or sick people stay out of danger until they can get them to a hospital. There, doctors take over and treat the patient.

Being an EMT requires a serious commitment to helping people. The training is intense. EMTs work incredibly hard and they have to be able to perform under heavy stress. After all, when someone's life is at stake, seconds matter.

All EMT trainees learn basic skills in handling **trauma** cases as well as basic medical response to heart attacks.

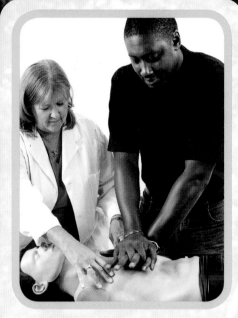

EMT training typically includes becoming certified in Cardiopulmonary Resuscitation or CPR. This life-saving procedure can restore a patient's breathing or heart function in an emergency.

EMERGENCY FACT

Because EMTs often lift people and equipment when responding to an emergency, they need to be physically fit and strong. They also need to be alert and poised under difficult working conditions.

People have gotten injured or unexpectedly sick since the beginning of time, but the organized and heroic help provided by EMTs is relatively new. Modern emergency response practices in the United States date back to the 1960s.

Prior to the late 1960s, there was no national organized first response plan to deal with **catastrophes**. If a person were hurt or dangerously ill, they had to get themselves to a hospital or find someone to take them.

Some hospitals began offering horse-drawn ambulance services as early as the 1860s.

The American Red Cross collected blood donations to help save injured soldiers.

EMERGENCY FACT

Valuable lessons in emergency response were learned in times of war. During wartime, military medical units were often under the gun to save soldiers wounded on the battlefield.

The national movement to using trained EMTs for first response came about due to a big increase in the number of people driving cars. As the number of people with cars rose, so too did the number of accidents. Those accidents resulted in serious injuries and even deaths. The victims were often too badly hurt to flag down help or drive themselves to the hospital.

When ambulances first became common in the United States, most drivers would simply transport the sick and injured to hospitals as quickly as possible. They did not give the victims any medical care. Even into the 1960s, ambulance drivers were rarely trained to perform even basic first aid.

EMERGENCY FACT

Seconds count! Sometimes a medical helicopter is used to transport people when there is a danger that the victim may not survive long enough to reach a hospital by regular ambulance.

Two landmark events helped form the foundation of today's modern EMT and paramedic forces in communities all across the nation.

1961 Alexandria Plan

In Alexandria, Virginia Dr. James Mills quit his regular practice to become an emergency room doctor. He formed a plan to hire an entire staff that only performed emergency care. The plan, known as the Alexandria Plan, was based on a sharp rise in serious trauma cases swamping the hospital's emergency room. The plan proved successful. Other hospitals soon began adopting it for themselves.

1966 National Academy of Science and the White Paper

National researchers produced a detailed study on the rise of serious injuries and deaths due to poor emergency care in the moments following serious accidents. The report was known as the White Paper. It showed that lives were lost because of poorly trained emergency workers.

EMERGENCY DEPARTME

Nearly 240 million calls are made to 9-1-1 every year in the United States.

Every minute counts when an EMT is responding to a medical emergency.

Emergencies can be as unpredictable as life itself. Accidents and health scares happen without warning at all hours of the day or night.

The time it takes an EMT to respond to an emergency depends on where it is happening. In cities, first responders often come from just blocks away. In remote, rural areas, EMTs may have to travel many miles to reach victims and transport them to hospitals.

EMTs sometimes have to help victims in places that are hard to reach. A person may be trapped under a collapsed building or have fallen ill during a wilderness hike. Getting help to people in dire situations is part of the EMTs job.

Wilderness EMTs

In some of the world's most rugged and remote locations, emergency response comes from specially trained Wilderness EMTs. These first responders often use helicopters to reach and transport people injured on mountainsides, miles from any roads or civilization.

From tornadoes to typhoons, heat waves to hailstorms, violent weather can create large-scale emergencies. When disasters happen and many people require rescue, EMTs and paramedics need help from neighboring departments.

In emergencies where many people have been hurt, the first EMTs to arrive may have to perform **triage**. They identify those victims most in need of immediate medical care.

Triage

Triage is a first-response tactic first used on the battlefield. Field medics had to quickly sort injuries based on their severity. This helped identify the most serious cases so they could be treated first. The less serious cases would be treated afterward.

On a battlefield, injured people may be taken to triage tents.

When multiple EMTs and paramedics respond to the same catastrophe, the highest-ranking first responder on the scene assumes the role of incident commander. He or she will direct and coordinate the rescue effort.

Some of the worst natural disasters have highlighted the need for well-trained EMTs.

EMTs usually work long shifts in between multiple days off. EMTs working within the ranks of a fire department can expect to be on duty for 24 hours at a time. They sometimes have two days off between each shift. This helps ensure they are available to respond to emergencies at all hours of the day or night.

In catastrophes where victims are not immediately visible, some EMTs may perform search and rescue. After a tornado hit Moore, Oklahoma in 2013, EMTs worked on search and rescue to deliver emergency treatment to people who were trapped.

The need for trained and capable EMTs and paramedics is only going to increase in the future.

One major reason for this change in the United States is that there will be more senior citizens among the population. There are more people over the age of 65 living in the U.S. than ever before.

Heart Attack Help

While responding to catastrophes is not a daily event for most EMTs, coming to the rescue of a senior citizen suffering from symptoms of a heart ailment is. Although it changes from region to region, chest pain or heart attack symptoms are among the leading reasons why people call 9-1-1 for help.

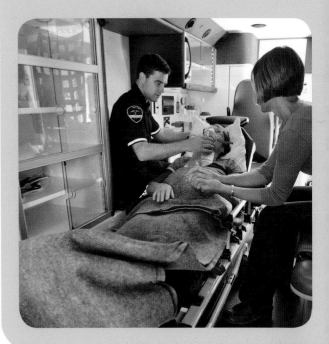

Emergency response will continue to evolve. EMTs need to undergo updated training as new medical practices or equipment become available.

EMTs and paramedics have to be ready for just about any situation a person can imagine. That constant state of readiness helps them deal with the tension of never knowing if that next call will be for a little boy's broken leg, a fire, a car crash, or even a natural disaster.

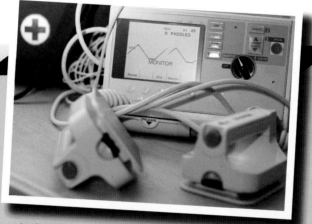

One medical device now commonly used by first responders is the heart defibrillator. The device sends an electrical pulse through a person's chest if they are in the midst of a serious heart ailment. The electrical pulse can restore a normal heartbeat. Once found only in hospital emergency rooms, defibrillators are now common in many public places. They are even on many airplanes.

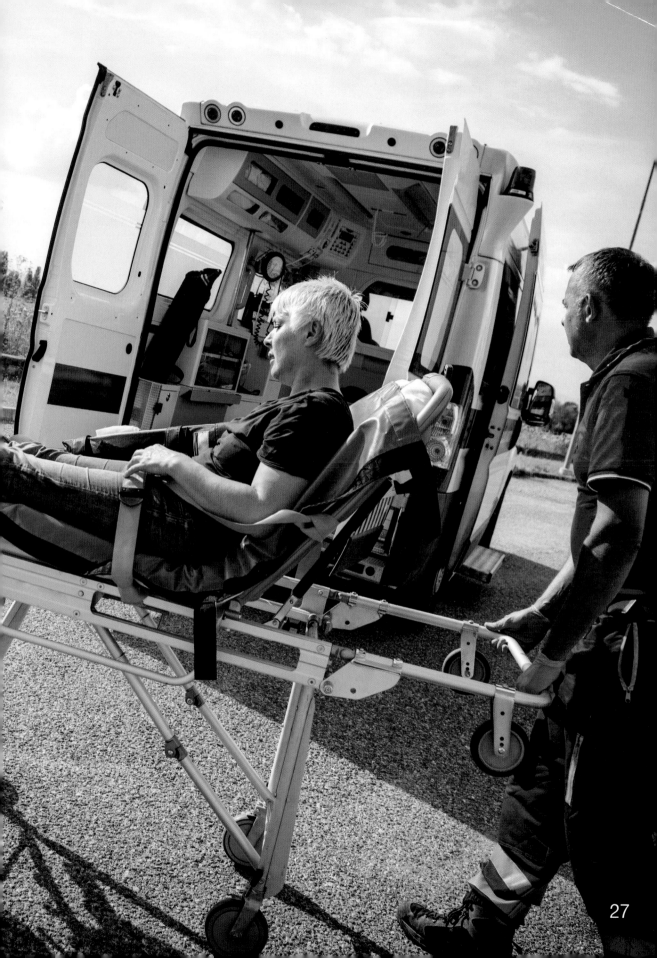

TIMELINE

1400s:
Spanish military uses special carts to carry wounded soldiers off battlefield.

1860s:
Hospitals begin using horse and buggy to bring sick or injured patients in for treatment.

1920s:
First automobile ambulances go into service.

1790s:
The personal doctor of French military leader Napoleon Bonaparte uses horse-drawn ambulance to give immediate treatment to wounded soldiers and uses triage tactics during battle.

1910:
Red Cross begins conducting first aid classes nationwide.

1939:
London hospitals coordinate emergency service plans in response to German air raids during World War II.

1950s:
Sharp increase in American car sales results in more accidental trauma cases.

1966:
White Paper governmental study shows urgent need to train ambulance workers and create the modern model of emergency response.

2000s:
EMTs routinely take part in elaborate disaster drills as part of their training after the September 11, 2001 terrorist attacks.

1961:
Alexandria Plan calls for dedicated emergency room staff and procedures.

1977:
The 6-point blue star of life becomes the official international symbol for EMTs.

GLOSSARY

catastrophes (kuh-TASS-truh-feez): terrible and sudden disasters

dispatcher (diss-PATCH-uhr): a person who relays emergency calls

distress (diss-TRESS): in need of help right away

efficiency (uh-FISH-uhn-see): making best use of time and effort

emergency (i-MUR-juhn-see): sudden and unexpected dangerous situation

rural (RUR-uhl): in the country, far from population centers

technician (tek-NISH-uhn): a person who works with specialized equipment

trauma (TRAW-muh): a severe physical wound or injury

triage (TREE-ahj): a method of quickly sorting injury victims for treatment

undergo (uhn-dur-GOH): to have to go through something

INDEX

SHOW WHAT YOU KNOW

1. What do you have to tell the dispatcher when you call 9-1-1?
2. Why do you think early ambulance drivers did not have
   medical training?
3. How have wars influenced emergency care?
4. What is one of the most common reasons people call 9-1-1?
5. Name three kinds of emergencies that EMTs respond to.

WEBSITES TO VISIT

www.emt-resources.com
www.ems.gov
www.911forkids.com